CHILD

CHILD

A LITERARY COMPANION

EDITED BY
HELEN HANDLEY AND ANDRA SAMELSON

PUSHCART PRESS

ISBN 0-916366-76-6

Distributed by W. W. Norton Co.
500 Fifth Ave, New York, NY 10110

Manufactured in The United States of America
by RAY FREIMAN and COMPANY, Stamford, Connecticut

This book is dedicated to
Miss Reed McLaurin Handley
Miss Lily Frances Henderson
and
Miss Allegra Samelson Wechsler

We were so appreciative of and encouraged by the very warm responses to CHILD, and we watched gratefully as new passages on the subject came in the mail from friends and strangers as far away as the midwest, the West coast, and even the Rocky Mountain area, and as close as next door in Manhattan. We received phone calls and inquiries from editors and individuals working at relevant publications as well, all of which encouraged us to reread and re-view the work we had done when we first assembled the quotations in CHILD. To our delight, the passages continued to yield insights to us and to take us on new journeys through the enchanted world of childhood and memory. Memories of our own childhood popped up with surprising energy: "You don't ask for memories, but they come anyway, like mosquitoes," says a character in a novel by Judith Freeman. So too do the excitement and energy generated by the concept of childhood "come anyway."

Recently, we came across a passage written by Wendy Lesser in which the subject of reading and childhood is examined, as well as the magical concept of time: "Things come around again, but they never come around in exactly the same form . . . " and words on a page read at different times say different things to us, though the actual printed page doesn't alter one iota.

Starting after page ninety-two, without altering the original quotations one iota, we have added to the printed pages of CHILD the sounds of new voices, which amplify and enrich our understanding of memory and childhood and which, we hope, will spark the reader's renewed interest in this extended life of CHILD.

H. H.   A. S.

F rom the vast storehouse of childhood experiences and memories and from the power of writers' inspirations, come the quotations gathered in this little anthology, focusing on the enduring child that is within each of us.

What vibrations and flashes of energy, what accuracy of feeling and of speech are to be found in these gems! From Rilke, Shelley, and Dickens to Colette and W. C. Fields, the voices are in turn nostalgic, humorous, contradictory, and wistful: there are quiet epiphanies and solemn reflections juxtaposed with wry truths and whimsical outbursts. And the more we read the more we may add our separate planes of time and varnishes of memory. Discovering the child within through these quotations is contagious and catches something deep that we do not want to give up.

This anthology is arranged according to general definitions and impressions of childhood, from expressions of innocence and youth, to loss of innocence and finally to the effort to recapture in adulthood that early self.

My gratitude goes to Bill Henderson of Pushcart Press, whose own spirit is radiant with youthful brightness and whose enthusiasm and encouragement have given shape to this book, and to William Cole, for his many children's books and for lending time and an ear.

H. H.

Some time ago, like many people who are not altogether at home in adulthood, I began to feel, as the Sufi expression goes, "plunged in galoshes up to my eyebrows". Bogged down by the general gravity of life and the seeming seriousness of making art, I felt I had lost my sense of play and resolved to recover it. Like Calder, who "decided to make a circus just for the fun of it," I started to make toys.

Soon my art studio was filled with my own windups, music boxes, whirligigs and playthings. I had thought these were for my enjoyment only, but I noticed that whenever I was visited by "serious" adults—gallery dealers and art critics, workmen and elderly relatives—we frequently found ourselves sitting on the floor playing with the toys and laughing.

This book was also made for "the fun of it", and came into being as a way of celebrating the spirit of childhood, that mysterious world always present within us however far away it may seem. It is often our willingness to play which brings back the freedom and wonder we once knew, just as the wish-fulfilling genie appeared when Aladdin rubbed his magic lamp. No matter what our age, it is never too late to have a happy childhood.

I offer my gratitude to Thinley Norbu Rinpoche who inspired the idea for this book through his example of ageless wisdom and joy.

A. S.

CHILD

Childhood—What was it, really? What *was* it, this childhood? How else to inquire about it than with this perplexed question—what was it—that burning, that amazement, that endless insufficiency, that sweet, that deep, that radiant feeling of tears welling up? What was it?

    RAINER MARIA RILKE

O Unicorn among the Cedars
To whom no magic charm can lead us,
White childhood moving like a sigh
Through the green woods.

    W. H. AUDEN

Bliss it was that dawn to be alive,
But to be young was very heaven!

    WILLIAM WORDSWORTH

That great Cathedral space which was childhood.

    VIRGINIA WOOLF

Babies are such a nice way to start people.

    DON HEROLD

In a secular age, children have become the last sacred objects.

JOSEPH EPSTEIN

We find delight in the beauty and happiness of children that makes the heart too big for the body.

RALPH WALDO EMERSON

One laugh of a child will make the holiest day more sacred still.

R. G. INGERSOLL

Ah! What would the world be to us
   If the children were no more?
We should dread the desert behind us
   Worse than the dark before.

HENRY WADSWORTH LONGFELLOW

Thou, straggler into loving arms,
Young climber up of knees,
When I forget thy thousand ways,
Then life and all shall cease.

MARY LAMB

Blessed be childhood, which brings down something of heaven into the midst of our rough earthliness.

HENRI-FRÉDÉRIC AMIEL

Where children are, there is the golden age.

NOVALIS

We could never have loved the earth so well if we had had no childhood in it.

GEORGE ELIOT

It is true that a child is always hungry all over; but he is also curious all over, and his curiosity is excited about as early as his hunger.

CHARLES DUDLEY WARNER

If a child is to keep alive his inborn sense of wonder, he needs the companionship of at least one adult who can share it, rediscovering with him the joy, excitement and mystery of the world we live in.

RACHEL CARSON

Children are remarkable for their intelligence and ardor, for their curiosity, their intolerance of shams, the clarity and ruthlessness of their vision.

ALDOUS HUXLEY

Only child life is real life.

GEORGE ORWELL

Know you what it is to be a child? It is to be something very different from the man of today; . . . it is to be so little that the elves can reach to whisper in your ear; it is to turn pumpkins into coaches, and mice into horses, lowness into loftiness, and nothing into everything, for each child has its fairy godmother in its soul.

PERCY BYSSHE SHELLEY

Never have ideas about children—and never have ideas *for* them.

D. H. LAWRENCE

Unlike grown-ups, children have little need to deceive themselves.

JOHANN WOLFGANG VON GOETHE

No one ever keeps a secret so well as a child.

VICTOR HUGO

The child does not know that men are not only bad
from good motives, but also often good from bad motives. Therefore the child has a hearty, healthy, un-
spoiled, and insatiable appetite for mere morality, for
the mere difference between a good little girl and a bad
little boy.

G. K. CHESTERTON

In the little world in which children have their existence, whosoever brings them up, there is nothing so
finely perceived and so finely felt, as injustice.

CHARLES DICKENS

Only children tell the truth.

DAVID BELASCO

Children, drunkards, and fools cannot lie.

RICHARD TAVERNER

Children are unpredictable. You never know what in-
consistency they're going to catch you in next.

FRANKLIN JONES

The gift of sudden insight is sometimes vouchsafed to
children.

THOMAS HARDY

Why, a four-year-old child could understand this report. Run out and find me a four-year-old child. I can't make head or tail out of it.

GROUCHO MARX

You cannot write for children . . . They're much too complicated. You can only write books that are of interest to them.

MAURICE SENDAK

All children smile in the same language.

BUMPERSTICKER

Every child is born a genius.

R. BUCKMINSTER FULLER

Children are the true connoisseurs. What's precious to them has no price—only value.

BEL KAUFMAN

If children grew up according to early indications, we should have nothing but geniuses.

JOHANN WOLFGANG VON GOETHE

Prodigy: a child who plays the piano when he ought to be in bed.

J. B. MORTON

I was not a child prodigy, because a child prodigy is a child who knows as much when it is a child as it does when it grows up.

WILL ROGERS

I am not young enough to know everything.

JAMES BARRIE

The only artists for whom I would make way are—children. For me the paintings of children belong side by side with the works of the masters.

HENRY MILLER

Every child is an artist. The problem is how to remain an artist once he grows up.

PABLO PICASSO

Unless [artists] can remember what it was to be a little boy, they are only half complete as artist and as man.

JAMES THURBER

The work of a child never fails to make appeal, to claim us, because it is always honest and sincere, always imbued with that magic certitude born of the direct, spontaneous approach.

HENRY MILLER

Children and lunatics cut the Gordian knot which the poet spends his life patiently trying to undo.

JEAN COCTEAU

My music is best understood by children and animals.

IGOR STRAVINSKY

As I watched her at play . . . it came to me that this child would pass through life as the angels live in heaven.

PEARL BUCK

It is truly wonderful to see what an effect being much in the air has upon this child; she is always a merry creature, but when she is much out of doors she seems to be almost crazy with happiness.

MARY WORDSWORTH

The enthusiasm which must be held in check was a great burden for a child's soul . . . to restrain meant to kill, to bury.

ANAÏS NIN

It is to be noted that children's plays are not sports, and should be regarded as their most serious actions.

MONTAIGNE

Childhood is frequently a solemn business for those inside it.

GEORGE F. WILL

. . . I don't believe in this chat about 'broken homes'. . . . Children make their own homes. They are at home in the womb, they are shaken out of that, they construct a new home of breast and cradle, they are hauled out of that, they make a new home of nursery, of playground, of society.

It is impossible to stop children making homes. They make them in woods and under tables, and round the garbage cans at the bottom of the alley. They make homes as they make flesh and make bone.

SYLVIA TOWNSEND WARNER

Children's rites are obscure, inexorably secret; calling, we know, for infinite cunning, for ordeal by fear and torture; requiring victims, summary executions, human sacrifices. The particular mysteries are impenetrable, the faithful speak a cryptic tongue; even if we were to chance to overhear unseen, we would be none the wiser. Their trade is all in postage stamps and marbles.

JEAN COCTEAU

As soon as a child has left the room his strewn toys become affecting.

RALPH WALDO EMERSON

In those days we had the savage's happy faculty of creating an object of worship out of almost any chance stick or stone . . . Our toys were almost idols. There was a glamour upon them such as we do not find in the more splendid possessions of our later years, as though a special light fell on them through some window of our hearts that is now blocked up forever.

ODELL SHEPARD

One of the greatest pleasures of childhood is found in the mysteries which it hides from the skepticism of the elders, and works up into small mythologies of its own.

OLIVER WENDELL HOLMES

Children are natural mythologists: they beg to be told tales, and love not only to invent but to enact falsehoods.

GEORGE SANTAYANA

When I was younger, I could remember anything, whether it had happened or not.

MARK TWAIN

'My children,' said an old man to his boys, scared by a figure in the dark entry, 'my children, you will never see anything worse than yourselves.'

RALPH WALDO EMERSON

There is no end to the violations committed by children on children, quietly talking alone.

ELIZABETH BOWEN

Children are such sticky things, 'specially after tea.

E. F. BENSON

Besides, they always smell of bread and butter.

LORD BYRON

Childhood smells of perfume and brownies.
    DAVID LEAVITT

It's odd how large a part food plays in memories of childhood. There are grown men and women who still shudder at the sight of spinach or turn away with loathing from stewed prunes and tapioca . . . Luckily, however, it's the good tastes one remembers best.
    CAROLINE LEJEUNE

Spinach: Divide into little piles. Rearrange again into new piles. After five or six maneuvers, sit back and say you are full.
    DELIA EPHRON

This would be a better world for children if parents had to eat the spinach.
    GROUCHO MARX

In general, my children refused to eat anything that hadn't danced on TV.
    ERMA BROMBECK

One child will not eat hot dogs, ice cream or cake, and asks for cereal. Sarah pours him out a bowl of Sugar Frosted Flakes, and a moment later he chokes. Sarah pounds him on the back and out spits a tiny green plastic snake with red glass eyes, the Surprise Gift. All the children want it.

PAMELA ZOLINE

"I'm so glad I don't like asparagus," said the small girl to a sympathetic friend. "Because, if I did, I should have to eat it, and I can't bear it."

LEWIS CARROLL

THE TOASTER
A silver-scaled Dragon with jaws flaming red
Sits at my elbow and toasts my bread.
I hand him fat slices, and then, one by one,
He hands them back when he sees they are done.

WILLIAM JAY SMITH

Children are poor men's riches.

THOMAS FULLER

Children are entitled to their otherness, as anyone is; and when we reach them, as we sometimes do, it is generally on a point of sheer delight, to us so astonishing, but to them so natural.

ALASTAIR REID

A child is an alienated creature.

SIMONE DE BEAUVOIR

Children are the sworn enemies of all conventionality.

ANONYMOUS

A strange child, perhaps, but I wouldn't give a pinch of dust for a child who was not strange. Is not every child strange, by adult accounting, if we could only learn to know it? If it has no strangeness, what is the use of it?

ROBERTSON DAVIES

The poetic transfiguration of childhood carried out by the bourgeois nineteenth century is so much stuff, there is nothing poetic about a child whatsoever. But it is true that for a child the world possesses a fascinating strangeness—always providing that he is lucky enough to be able to gaze upon it and explore it.

SIMONE DE BEAUVOIR

The entry of a child into any situation changes the whole situation.
    IRIS MURDOCK

Childish fantasy, like the sheath over the bud, not only protects but curbs the terrible budding spirit, protects not only innocence from the world, but the world from the power of innocence.
    ELIZABETH BOWEN

Childhood is the sleep of reason.
    JEAN JACQUES ROUSSEAU

Children use the fist
Until they are of age to use the brain.
    ELIZABETH BARRETT BROWNING

The age of a child is inversely correlated with the size of animals it prefers.
    DESMOND MORRIS

Young people are always more given to admiring what is gigantic than what is reasonable.
    EUGENE DELACROIX

A child's love is water in a basket.
SPANISH PROVERB

Children sometimes flatter old people, but they never love them.
FRENCH PROVERB

Women make us poets, children make us philosophers.
MALCOLM DE CHAZAL

The period of childhood is a stage on which time and space become entangled.
YUKIO MISHIMA

Childhood has no forebodings; but then, it is soothed by no memories of outlived sorrow.
GEORGE ELIOT

Children have neither past nor future; and that which seldom happens to us, they rejoice in the present.
JEAN DE LA BRUYÈRE

The lost child cries, but still he catches fireflies.
RYUSUI YOSHIDA

I am certain that children always know more than they are able to tell, and that makes the big difference between them and adults, who, at best, know only a fraction of what they say. The reason is simply that children know everything with their whole beings, while we know it only with our heads.

JACQUES LUSSEYRAN

Childhood is the kingdom where nobody dies.

EDNA ST. VINCENT MILLAY

Children sweeten labours, but they make misfortunes more bitter; they increase the cares of life, but they mitigate the remembrance of death.

FRANCIS BACON

A child is not frightened at the thought of being patiently transmuted into an old man.

ANTOINE DE ST. EXUPÉRY

Old age lives minutes slowly, hours quickly; childhood chews hours and swallows minutes.

MALCOLM DE CHAZAL

Childhood is not only the childhood we really had but also the impressions we formed of it in our adolescence and maturity. That is why childhood seems so long. Probably every period of life is multiplied by our reflections upon it in the next.

CESARE PAVESE

Somehow, when you're a child, you simply accept each turn of events as it comes, as if there is no other way for the world to be.

ISABEL HUGGAN

Children's talent to endure stems from their ignorance of alternatives.

MAYA ANGELOU

Making terms with reality, with things as they are, is a full-time business for the child.

MILTON R. SAPIRSTEIN

To children childhood holds no particular advantage.

KATHLEEN NORRIS

Youth, even in its sorrows, has a brilliance of its own.

VICTOR HUGO

At eight or nine, I suppose, intelligence is no more than a small spot of light on the floor of a large and murky room.

H. L. MENCKEN

How is it that little children are so intelligent and men so stupid? It must be education that does it.

ALEXANDRE DUMAS *FILS*

What a distressing contrast there is between the radiant intelligence of the child and the feeble mentality of the average adult.

SIGMUND FREUD

I was always running; the whole of my childhood was spent running. Only I was not running to catch hold of something. That is a notion for grown-ups and not the notion of a child. I was running to meet everything that was visible, and everything that I could not yet see. I traveled from assurance to assurance, as though I were running a race in relays.

JACQUES LUSSEYRAN

A man can never quite understand a boy, even when he has been the boy.

G. K. CHESTERTON

A boy becomes an adult three years before his parents think he does, and about two years after he thinks he does.

GENERAL LEWIS B. HERSHEY

The difference between a childhood and a boyhood must be this: our childhood is what we alone have had; our boyhood is what any boy in our environment would have had.

JOHN UPDIKE

I only know two sorts of boys: Mealy boys and beef-faced boys.

CHARLES DICKENS

A boy's will is the wind's will,
And the thoughts of youth are long, long thoughts.

HENRY WADSWORTH LONGFELLOW

Boys like romantic tales; but babies like realistic tales—because they find them romantic.

G. K. CHESTERTON

Every well-dressed boy owned a sailor suit.

WALT KELLY

Every boy, in his heart, would rather steal second base than an automobile.

JUSTICE TOM CLARK

Boys will be boys.

BULWER-LYTTON

Boys do not grow up gradually. They move forward in spurts like the hands of clocks in railway stations.

CYRIL CONNOLLY

Boys are capital fellows in their own way, among their mates; but they are unwholesome companions for grown people.

CHARLES LAMB

Every time a boy shows his hands, someone suggests that he wash them.

E. W. HOWE

A boy is, of all wild beasts, the most difficult to manage.

PLATO

A growing boy has a wolf in his belly.
  GERMAN PROVERB

A boy is a cross between a god and a goat.
  ANONYMOUS

Boyhood is a summer sun.
  EDGAR ALLAN POE

O see the poles of promise in the boys.
  DYLAN THOMAS

You may chisel a boy into shape, as you would a rock, or hammer him into it if he be of a better kind, as you would a piece of bronze. But you cannot hammer a girl into anything. She grows as a flower does.
  JOHN RUSKIN

Playmates of my childhood, girls, did I not love you? How I rushed to meet you—and you too were breath-less, your hot fragrance rising toward me like midsum-mer fields of clover . . . How could I not have loved you?
  RAINER MARIA RILKE

It is only rarely that one can see in a little boy the promise of a man, but one can almost always see in a little girl the threat of a woman.

ALEXANDRE DUMAS

I am an only child. I have one sister.

WOODY ALLEN

Girls are said to be sooner women than boys are men.

SAMUEL RICHARDSON

Whatever good there is in small boys is usually based upon their admiration for girls of their own age.

ARTHUR BRISBANE

Young girls are the chatelaines of truth; they must see that it is protected, that the guilty lead the life of the guilty, even if the world rocks on its foundations.

JEAN GIRAUDOUX

It is easier to guard a sack of fleas than a girl in love.

JEWISH PROVERB

Girls and glass are always in danger.
   ITALIAN PROVERB

The whisper of a pretty girl can be heard further than
the roar of a lion.
   ARAB PROVERB

Oh, you mysterious girls, when you are fifty-two we
shall find you out. You must come into the open then.
   J. M. BARRIE

What is more enchanting than the voices of young
people when you can't hear what they say?
   LOGAN PEARSALL SMITH

Babies do not want to hear about babies; they like to be
told of giants and castles.
   DR. SAMUEL JOHNSON

A child, when it begins to speak, learns what it is that
it knows.
   JOHN HALL WHEELOCK

Children have wide ears and long tongues.
THOMAS FULLER

Teach your child to hold his tongue; he'll learn fast enough to speak.
BENJAMIN FRANKLIN

When children are doing nothing, they are doing mischief.
HENRY FIELDING

In silence I must take my seat . . .
I must not speak a useless word
For children must be seen not heard.
B. W. BELLAMY

Children should neither be seen nor heard from—ever again.
W. C. FIELDS

For children is there any happiness which is not also noise?
FREDERICK W. FABER

When children sound silly, you will always find that it is in imitation of their elders.

ERNEST DINNET

My theory is that children are the grown-ups. They are very calculating by nature . . . I went to Macy's to see Santa Claus and to listen to the kids. . . . It was like a business convention at the Statler Hilton.

RICHARD LINDNER

The business of being a child interests a child not at all. Children very rarely play at being other children.

DAVID HOLLOWAY

To Tennessee Williams, children were "no-neck monsters," while William Wordsworth apotheosized the newborn infant as a "Mighty Prophet! Seer Blest!" Most adults know the truth is somewhere in between.

ELOISE SALHOLZ

I must have been an insufferable child; all children are.

GEORGE BERNARD SHAW

I was born in a very fortunate age. The term 'juvenile delinquent' wasn't thought of. We were just known as pests.

REV. JOHN CARMEL HEENAN

Children are overwhelming, supercilious. passionate, envious, inquisitive, egotistical, idle, fickle, timid, intemperate, liars and dissemblers; they laugh and weep easily, are excessive in their joys and sorrows, and that about the most trifling subjects; they bear no pain, but like to inflict it on others; already they are men.

JEAN DE LA BRUYÈRE

. . . children are capable, in the midst of the gentlest banter, of twisting one's finger nearly out of its socket, because they have developed their heedless affections on dolls, which never talk back.

RAINER MARIA RILKE

Any man who hates children can't be all bad.

W. C. FIELDS

Is this your basketball? It seems to have fallen under my tire several times.

W. C. FIELDS

Inside the illustration, a sign reads: WEEK DAY MEETINGS FOR THE YOUNG COME AS YOU ARE

They lie flat on their noses at first in what appears to be a drunken slumber, then flat on their backs kicking and screaming, demanding impossibilities in a foreign language. They are human nature in essence, without conscience, without pity, without love, without a trace of consideration for others—just one seething cauldron of primitive appetites.

KATHERINE ANNE PORTER

The life of children, as much as that of intemperate men, is wholly governed by their desires.

ARISTOTLE

Aren't children lovable because they're falling down all the time and have little bodies with the heads too big? Didn't Walt Disney know all about this when he did the seven dwarfs? And these funny little dogs that people have—they're lovable because they're imperfect.

JOSEPH CAMPBELL

Being constantly with children was like wearing a pair of shoes that were expensive and too small. She couldn't bear to throw them out, but they gave her blisters.

BERYL BAINBRIDGE

I keep as far from them as possible. I don't like the size of them; the scale is all wrong. The heads tend to be too big for the bodies and the hands and feet are a disaster and they keep falling into things, and the nakedness of their bad character. . . . You see, we adults have learned how to disguise our terrible characters but a child . . . well, it's like a grotesque drawing of us.

GORE VIDAL

Ah, the patter of little feet around the house. There's nothing like having a midget for a butler.

W. C. FIELDS

I love children. Especially when they cry—for then someone takes them away.

NANCY MITFORD

A child is a curly, dimpled lunatic.

RALPH WALDO EMERSON

The trouble with children is that they are not returnable.

QUENTIN CRISP

There are two classes of travel—first class, and with children.

ROBERT BENCHLEY

I have been assured by a very knowing American of my acquaintance in London, that a young healthy child well nursed is at a year old a most delicious, nourishing, and wholesome food, whether stewed, roasted, baked or boiled, and I make no doubt that it will equally serve in a fricassee, or a ragout.

JONATHAN SWIFT

By the time the youngest children have learned to keep the house tidy, the oldest grandchildren are on hand to tear it to pieces.

CHRISTOPHER MORLEY

People who say they sleep like a baby usually don't have one.

LEO BURKE

My wife and I just had a baby, and there's nothing re-laxed about them. They're like these little tense things who scream in order to fall asleep. Just like adults, only more direct.

IAN SHOALES

Babies on airplanes that howl all through the flight I certainly do *not* approve of. There should be special baby compartments. I think they should put the cigarette smokers and babies together and see who drives the other crazy quicker.

JOHN SIMON

Cleaning your house while your kids are still growing is like shovelling the walk before it stops snowing.

PHYLLIS DILLER

It was no wonder that people were so horrible when they started life as children.

KINGSLEY AMIS

Children are a torment and nothing more.

LEO TOLSTOY

I detest a child that is wise too soon.

ERASMUS

The fault no child ever loses is the one he was most punished for.

CESARE BECCARIA

You Americans do not rear children, you *incite* them,
you give them food and shelter and applause.
RANDALL JARRELL

He that spareth his rod hateth his son.
OLD TESTAMENT

Children aren't happy with nothing to ignore,
And that's what parents were created for.
OGDEN NASH

Better the child should cry than the father.
GERMAN PROVERB

Diogenes struck the father when the son swore.
ROBERT BURTON

Children have more need of models than of critics.
JOSEPH JOUBERT

Better a little chiding than a great deal of heartbreak.
WILLIAM SHAKESPEARE

Speak roughly to your little boy,
And beat him when he sneezes:
He only does it to annoy,
Because he knows it teases.

    LEWIS CARROLL

A spoilt child never loves its mother.

    SIR HENRY TAYLOR

What the mother sings to the cradle goes all the way
down to the coffin.

    HENRY WARD BEECHER

You don't have to deserve your mother's love. You have
to deserve your father's. He's more particular.

    ROBERT FROST

Where parents do too much for their children, the children will not do much for themselves.

    ELBERT HUBBARD

Respect the child. Be not too much his parent. Trespass
not on his solitude.

    RALPH WALDO EMERSON

The wildest colts make the best horses.
PLUTARCH

Children begin by loving their parents. After a time they judge them. Rarely, if ever, do they forgive them.
OSCAR WILDE

The monsters of our childhood do not fade away, neither are they ever wholly monstrous. But neither, in my experience, do we ever reach a plane of detachment regarding our parents, however wise and old we may become. To pretend otherwise is to cheat.
JOHN LE CARRÉ

All children alarm their parents, if only because you are forever expecting to encounter yourself.
GORE VIDAL

Don't give a child a knife.
GREEK PROVERB

Nervous breakdowns are hereditary. We get them from our children.
GRAFFITO.

If you wish your children to be well, let them be always three-tenths hungry and cold.

ARTHUR MOULE

From the day your baby is born, you must teach him to do without things. Children today love luxury too much. They have execrable manners, flaunt authority, have no respect for their elders. They no longer rise when their parents or teachers enter the room. What kind of awful creatures will they be when they grow up?

SOCRATES

Waiting to be whipped is the most uninteresting period of boyhood life.

JOSH BILLINGS

The discontented child cries for toasted snow.

ARAB PROVERB

It is cruel to compliment children since they mistake flattery for truth.

ANN RADCLIFFE

My father was frightened of his mother. I was frightened of my father, and I'm damned well going to make sure that my children are frightened of me.

GEORGE V

Child! Do not throw this book about!
Refrain from the unholy pleasure
Of cutting all the pictures out!

HILAIRE BELLOC

There never was child so lovely but his mother was glad to get him asleep.

RALPH WALDO EMERSON

It is impossible for any woman to love her children twenty-four hours a day.

MILTON R. SAPIRSTEIN

If there were no schools to take the children away from home part of the time, the insane asylums would be filled with mothers.

E. W. HOWE

When a woman is twenty, a child deforms her; when she is thirty, he preserves her; and when forty, he makes her young again.

LÉON BLUM

The most important thing a father can do for his children is to love their mother.

REV. THEODORE HESBURGH

Who takes the child by the hand, takes the mother by the heart.

DANISH PROVERB

There's only one pretty child in the world, and every mother has it.

J. C. BRIDGE

My mother loved children—she would have given anything if I had been one.

GROUCHO MARX

The fundamental defect of fathers is that they want their children to be a credit to them.

BERTRAND RUSSELL

There are some extraordinary fathers, who seem during the whole course of their lives, to be giving their children reasons for being consoled at their death.

JEAN DE LA BRUYÈRE

The longer I live the more keenly I feel that whatever was good enough for our fathers is not good enough for us.

OSCAR WILDE

Schoolmasters and parents exist to be grown out of.

JOHN WOLFENDEN

The time not to become a father is eighteen years before a war.

E. B. WHITE

The real menace in dealing with a five-year-old is that in no time at all you begin to sound like a five-year-old.

JEAN KERR

If there is anything we wish to change in the child, we should first examine it and see whether it is not something that could be better changed in ourselves.

C. G. JUNG

A torn jacket is soon mended; but hard words bruise the heart of a child.

HENRY WADSWORTH LONGFELLOW

Give a little love to a child, and you get a great deal back.

JOHN RUSKIN

A child's spirit is like a child, you can never catch it by running after it; you must stand still, and, for love, it will soon itself come back.

ARTHUR MILLER

A child hasn't a grown-up person's appetite for affection. A little of it goes a long way with them; and they like a good imitation of it better than the real thing, as every nurse knows.

GEORGE BERNARD SHAW

To neglect children is to murder them.

DANIEL DEFOE

Every person needs recognition. It is expressed cogently by the child who says, "Mother, let's play darts. I'll throw the darts and you say 'wonderful.'"

M. DALE BAUGHAM

A child is fed with milk and praise.

MARY LAMB

You can do anything with children if you only play with them.

OTTO VON BISMARCK

I do not teach children, I give them joy.

ISADORA DUNCAN

Perhaps a child who is fussed over gets a feeling of destiny; he thinks he is in the world for something important and it gives him drive and confidence.

DR. BENJAMIN SPOCK

Allow children to be happy their own way; for what better way will they ever find?

DR. SAMUEL JOHNSON

The best way to give advice to your children is to find out what they want and advise them to do it.

HARRY TRUMAN

There are only two lasting bequests we can hope to give our children. One of these is roots; the other, wings.

HODDING CARTER

Do not try to produce an ideal child; it would find no fitness in this world.

HERBERT SPENCER

Perhaps host and guest is really the happiest relation for father and son.

EVELYN WAUGH

Who of us is mature enough for offspring before the offspring themselves arrive? The value of marriage is not that adults produce children but that children produce adults.

PETER DE VRIES

I think most people should be discouraged from having children, because most people have no gift for parenthood. Most parents realize this eventually. The children, of course, realize it right away.

GORE VIDAL

Train up a child in the way he should go and when he is old he will not depart from it.

PROVERBS

What you have inherited from your father, you must earn over again for yourselves, or it will not be yours.

JOHANN WOLFGANG VON GOETHE

It is hard to grow up in the shadow of such a great oak.

RANDOLPH CHURCHILL

If you refuse to be made straight when you are green you will not be made straight when you are dry.

AFRICAN PROVERB

It is not easy to straighten in the oak the crook that grew in the sapling.

GAELIC PROVERB

Nothing would induce me to go over my childhood days again. I thought I was happy because my mother said I was.

REV. H. R. L. SHEPPARD

Some people do not make good children. They should spring upon the world fully grown, preferably with a gin and tonic in hand, and conversation in full swing, a camera equipped with sound on the premises to record the event.

MARGARET MORLEY

It is . . . sometimes easier to head an institute for the study of child guidance than it is to turn one brat into a decent human being.

JOSEPH WOOD KRUTCH

Give your child plenty of time with nothing in particular to do. Serve your child a drupe or a legume every day. Make sure that your income fluctuates significantly. Do not videotape your child in the bathtub. Do not name your child after a Scandinavian deity, or any aspect of the weather. Encourage your child to keep looking for something until he finds it. Once a year, change the family's destination in the middle of a trip. Conspire with your child. Pay no heed to helpful hints. Never call anything with fewer than four legs a puppy.

DANIEL MENAKER

Just think of the tragedy of teaching children not to doubt.

CLARENCE DARROW

Give me the children until they are seven and anyone may have them afterwards.

ST. FRANCIS XAVIER

Give us the child for eight years, and it will be a Bolshevist forever.

NIKOLAI LENIN

Children have never been very good at listening to their elders, but they have never failed to imitate them.

JAMES BALDWIN

Is it not strange that he who has no children brings them up so well?

CONFUCIUS

If we do not keep on speaking terms with children, we cease to be men, and become merely machines for eating and earning money.

JOHN UPDIKE

Parents who expect gratitude from their children (there are even some who insist on it) are like usurers who gladly risk their capital if only they receive interest.

FRANZ KAFKA

Reasoning with a child is fine, if you can reach the child's reason without destroying your own.

JOHN MASON BROWN

To talk to a child, to fascinate him, is much more difficult than to win an electoral victory. But it is also more rewarding.

COLETTE

The only rational way of educating a child is to be an example—of what to avoid, if one can't be the other sort.

ALBERT EINSTEIN

Better to be driven out from among men than to be disliked of children.

R. H. DANA

People with bad consciences always fear the judgment of children.

MARY MCCARTHY

They will judge you as a person who . . . had a light step, a long look, a comfortable way of laughing, who could hoist one into a tree and lift one down again at the right moment, whose coat's shoulder had a particular smell. That is how. I don't think you need worry yourself over that.

SYLVIA TOWNSEND WARNER

You can't be too careful what you tell a child because you never know what he'll take hold of and spend the rest of his life remembering you by.

FREDERICK BUECHNER

Romance fails us and so do friendships, but the relationship of parent and child, less noisy than all others, remains indelible and indestructible, the strongest relationship on earth.

THEODOR REIK

I had been brought up with the phrase "That's your father in you" ringing in my ears every time I did something wrong, every time I told a lie, pilfered or stayed out too late. When I met my father I liked him much better than I really expected to.

HOWARD LINDSAY

All women become like their mothers. That is their tragedy. No man does. That is his.

OSCAR WILDE

The childhood shows the man,
As morning shows the day.

JOHN MILTON

I don't believe for a moment that all the clues to character are to be found in childhood. . . . All this militarization of childhood, all the menacing idiocy, erotic tension (at ten we all lusted for our female teachers) had not affected our ethics much, or our aesthetics—or our ability to love and suffer.

JOSEPH BRODSKY

On the one hand, of course, the Freudian legacy assures us that our childhoods are with us for life: we are what they made us; we cannot lose their gains, or be compensated for their losses. On the other, children themselves have been devalued: we know them for the little beasts they are (a knowledge greatly amplified since 1945 by the forcible reintroduction of a servantless middle class to its offspring), and nobody would pretend there was anything angelic about them, so that one of the major illusions of the Romantic movement has thereby quietly disappeared, like knives and forks from a university refectory.

PHILIP LARKIN

Childhood decides.

JEAN PAUL SARTRE

The proper time to influence the character of a child is about a hundred years before he is born.

W. R. INGE

The child must teach the man.

JOHN GREENLEAF WHITTIER

The thing that impresses me most about America is the way parents obey their children.

EDWARD VIII

The child of Themistocles governed his mother;
The mother governed her husband;
The husband governed Athens;
Athens governed the world.
Therefore, Themistocles' child governed the world.

ANONYMOUS

Childhood used to end with the discovery that there is no Santa Claus. Nowadays, it too often ends when the child gets his first adult, the way Hemingway got his first rhino, with the difference that the rhino was charging Hemingway, whereas the adult is usually running from the child.

JAMES THURBER

We had bad luck with our kids—they've all grown up.

CHRISTOPHER MORLEY

Childhood candor . . . shall I ever find you again?

LEO TOLSTOY

But still I dream that somewhere there must be
The spirit of a child that waits for me.
    BAYARD TAYLOR

Ah! happy years! Once more who would not be a boy!
    LORD BYRON

Our dearest, our white youth,
ah, our white, our snow-white youth,
that is infinite, and yet so brief,
spreads over us like the wings of an archangel! . . .
It is forever exhausted, forever loving;
and it melts and faints among white horizons,
Ah, it goes there, is lost in white horizons,
goes forever.
    C. P. CAVAFY

Alas, that Spring should vanish with the Rose!
That Youth's sweet-scented Manuscript should close.
    EDWARD FITZGERALD

One stops being a child when one realizes that telling
one's trouble does not make it better.
    CESARE PAVESE

I was fourteen, and abruptly at the end of the holidays some soft, almost physical appendage of childhood seems to have fallen away, like the tail of a tadpole, and I would never be quite the same again.

PAUL MULDOON

Ah! Why have I lost the eyes of childhood?

ADJUTOR RIVARD

Someone too early abandoned the task of being a child.

TOMAS TRANSTROMER

Ah, there are no children nowadays.

MOLIÈRE

We see these adolescents mourning for a lost childhood.

DAVID ELKIND

There is always one moment in childhood when the door opens and lets in the future.

GRAHAM GREENE

When I was a child, I spake as a child, I understood as a child, I thought as a child: but when I became a man, I put away childish things.

CORINTHIANS

She felt vaguely that she had given away her childhood that night. She had given it to him or he had taken it from her, and made it into something wonderful. In a way, her life was his now.

BETTY SMITH

In the lost childhood of Judas
Christ was betrayed.

GEORGE WILLIAM RUSSELL

If youth is a defect, it is one that we outgrow too soon.

ROBERT LOWELL

When childhood dies, its corpses are called adults and they enter society, one of the politer names of hell. That is why we dread children, even if we love them. They show us the state of our decay.

BRIAN ALDISS

In the child, happiness dances; in the man, at most it smiles or weeps.

CONRAD RICHTER

The child sees everything which has to be experienced and learned as a doorway. So does the adult. But what to the child is an entrance is to the adult only a passage.

FRIEDRICH NIETZSCHE

Childhood is the world of miracle and wonder; as if creation rose, bathed in light, out of the darkness, utterly new and fresh and astonishing. The end of childhood is when things cease to astonish us. When the world seems familiar, when one has got used to existence, one has become an adult.

EUGÈNE IONESCO

Children are born optimists, and we slowly educate them out of their heresy.

LOUISE IMOGEN GUINEY

Not to expose your true feelings to an adult seems to be instinctive from the age of seven or eight onwards.

GEORGE ORWELL

Childhood is the country that produces the most nostalgic, contentious, and opinionated exiles.

RICHARD EDER

Sons forget what grandsons wish to remember.
ALICE ROSSI

. . . give me back
my ancient soul of a child,
mellowed with legends,
with the feathered cap,
and the wooden sword.
GARCIA LORCA

There was a child went forth every day;
And the first object he look'd upon, that object he became;
And that object became part of him for the day, or a
certain part of the day, or for many years, or stretching
cycles of years.
WALT WHITMAN

For the euphoria which we endeavor to reach by these
means is nothing other than the mood of a period of
life . . . the mood of our childhood, when we were ig-
norant of the comic, when we were incapable of jokes
and when we had no need of humour to make us feel
happy in our life.
SIGMUND FREUD

I always feel that we keep our childhood locked inside, in a hidden cabinet. We carry it with us, and we see it most clearly in those moments when we are able to feel passionately responsive to children. Some people, I think, have buried their childhood, or they have done something terrible: They have murdered it. These are the sad characters one sees passing by an innocent face and open little arms with indifference; or else with a bad conscience.

MAGDA VON HATTINBERG

Youth sees too far to see how near it is
To seeing farther.

EDWIN ARLINGTON ROBINSON

Youth is not a time of life; it is a state of mind.

SAMUEL ULLMAN

Those who love the young best stay young longest.

EDGAR I. FRIEDENBERG

To love and to please is to be always young.

LOUISE HONORINE DE CHOISEUL

Youth! Stay close to the young, and a little rubs off.
    ALAN JAY LERNER

Except ye be converted, and become as little children,
ye shall not enter into the kingdom of heaven.
    ST. MATTHEW

Keep true to the dreams of thy youth.
    JOHANN SCHILLER

It is better to waste one's youth than to do nothing with
it at all.
    GEORGES COURTELINE

Youth, I loved you; those loveliest years, when
Brief as they were, love was my only occupation.
    SOPHIE DE LA BRICHE HOUDETOT

Forgotten impressions of childhood and youth came
back to me—all those indescribable effects wrought by
colour, shadow, sunlight, green hedges, and songs of
birds upon the soul just opening to poetry. I became
again young, wondering, and simple, as candour and
ignorance are simple.
    HENRI-FRÉDÉRIC AMIEL

Youth had been a habit of hers for so long, that she could not part with it.

RUDYARD KIPLING

A man is not to aim at innocence, any more than he is to aim at hair; but he is to keep it.

RALPH WALDO EMERSON

In the man whose childhood has known caresses and kindness, there is always a fiber of memory that can be touched to gentle issues.

GEORGE ELIOT

A happy childhood can't be cured. Mine'll hang around my neck like a rainbow, that's all, instead of a noose.

HORTENSE CALISHER

Youth lasts much longer than young people think.

COMTESSE DIANE

The morn and liquid dew of youth.

WILLIAM SHAKESPEARE

Youth is something very new: twenty years ago, no one mentioned it.

COCO CHANEL

Everyone's youth is a dream, a form of chemical madness.

F. SCOTT FITZGERALD

Youth means love.

ROBERT BROWNING

A youth without fire is followed by an old age without experience.

CHARLES CALEB COLTON

No time to marry, no time to settle down;
I'm a young woman, and I ain't done runnin' around.

BESSIE SMITH

I flutter like a child after her mother.

SAPPHO

Men are but children of a larger growth.

JOHN DRYDEN

Youth is unending intoxication; it is a fever of the mind.

LA ROCHEFOUCAULD

So, like a forgotten fire, a childhood can always flare up again within us.

GASTON BACHELARD

In every man there lies hidden a child between five and eight years old, the age at which naiveté comes to an end. It is this child whom one must detect in that intimidating man with his long beard, bristling eyebrows, heavy mustache, and weighty look—a captain. Even he conceals, and not at all deep down, the youngster, the booby, the little rascal, out of whom age has made this powerful monster.

PAUL VALÉRY

Everyone knows a good deal about one child—himself.

BRAD CARTER

. . . we need to return to the mythologies that today we only teach children.

ROBERT BLY

Some people, you know, are never children, or only briefly. Some have their childhoods much later in their lives. It is certainly not the exclusive privilege of the very young, but merely that time when one feels the greatest awe, terror, and confidence in the universe and in oneself.

ISAK DINESEN

. . . some day you will be old enough to start reading fairy tales again.

C. S. LEWIS

Little Red Riding Hood was my first love. I felt that if I could have married Little Red Riding Hood, I should have known perfect bliss.

CHARLES DICKENS

Baseball gave me a sense of direction. It opened a world of several hundred valiant characters and situations that changed from day to day. Once I entered that world there was no tiptoeing back out to simpler realms where Pooh bears dipped into honey pots and wizards worked in Oz. I was in an enchanted land of my own, and what's more, I could read new stories about it every morning.

WILLIAM K. ZINSSER

Child's play! Those gentlemen the critics often say that my pictures resemble the scribbles and messes of children. I hope they do! The pictures that my little boy Felix paints are often better than mine, because mine have been filtered through the brain, which regrettably I cannot always avoid because sometimes I work too much.

PAUL KLEE

There exists a passion for comprehension, just as there exists a passion for music. That passion is rather common in children, but gets lost in most people later on.

ALBERT EINSTEIN

Genius is childhood recaptured at will.

CHARLES BAUDELAIRE

I think like a genius, I write like a distinguished author, and I speak like a child.

VLADIMIR NABOKOV

I sometimes ask myself how did it come that I was the one to develop the theory of relativity. The reason, I think, is that a normal adult never stops to think about problems of space and time. These are things which he has thought of as a child. But my intellectual development was retarded, as a result of which I began to wonder about space and time only when I had already grown up. Naturally, I could go deeper into the problem than a child with normal abilities.

ALBERT EINSTEIN

Mystics pass for the most part through a period of spiritual childhood and hard education, marked by the child's intensity of feeling and distorted scale of values, its abounding vitality, dramatic instinct and lack of control.

MARIANNE MOORE

What can I say to you? I am perhaps the oldest musician in the world. I am an old man, but in many senses a very young man. And this is what I want you to be, young, young all your life, and to say things to the world that are true.

PABLO CASALS

I'm not really a young man but I'm a man who's still young. Youth doesn't mean much. I'm very young, whereas all my contemporaries in Stampa are old men, because they've accepted old age. Their lives are already in the past. But mine is in the future. It's only now that I can envisage the possibility of trying to start on my life's work.

ALBERTO GIACOMETTI

The thing is to become a master and in your old age to acquire the courage to do what children did when they knew nothing.

HENRY MILLER

Children, like animals, use all their senses to discover the world. Then artists come along and discover it the same way all over again.

EUDORA WELTY

Artists don't seek reasons. They are all by definition children and vice versa.

NED ROREM

I remember when I was very young and I saw the circus. I thought: "How can life be like that? Can you live that way and always pay attention to the absurd?" I try to create my art with this in mind.

PAT OLESZKO

I decided to make a circus just for the fun of it.

ALEXANDER CALDER

The maturity of man—that means to have reacquired the seriousness that one had as a child at play.

FRIEDRICH NIETZSCHE

Because of my willingness to play on the surface, the work underneath can then take place.

JOSEPH CHILTON PEARCE

It is a happy talent to know how to play.

RALPH WALDO EMERSON

The true object of human life is play. Earth is a task garden; heaven is a playground.

G. K. CHESTERTON

In the sun that is young once only,
Time let me play and be
Gold in the mercy of his means.

DYLAN THOMAS

The serious side of life is the toy of the adult. Only it is not to be compared with the sensible things that fill a nursery.

KARL KRAUS

The adult on the verge of death may be permitted a return to childhood, as is the Japanese kamikaze flier who is given toys to play with.

MARGARET MEAD

Life should begin with age and its privileges and accumulations, and end with youth and its capacity to splendidly enjoy such advantages.

MARK TWAIN

We do not have a childhood, a maturity, an old age: several times during our lives we have our seasons, but their course is not well known: it is not clearly laid out.

JULES RENARD

Youth hasn't got anything to do with chronological age. It's times of hope and happiness.

WALLACE STEGNER

We are always the same age inside.

GERTRUDE STEIN

Indeed, now that I come to think of it, I never really feel grown-up at all. Perhaps this is because childhood, catching our imagination when it is fresh and tender, never lets go of us.

J.B. PRIESTLEY

The character we exhibit in the latter half of our life need not necessarily be, though it often is, our original character, developed further, dried up, exaggerated, or diminished: it can be its exact opposite, like a suit worn inside out.

MARCEL PROUST

Do engine drivers, I wonder, eternally wish they were small boys?

FLANN O'BRIEN

Adults are obsolete children.

DR. SEUSS

What is an adult? A child blown up by age.

SIMONE DE BEAUVOIR

My father is a great big child whom I had when I was a boy.

ALEXANDRE DUMAS *FILS*

. . . My second childhood of seeing and learning, my second life, so far away from my first.

V. S. NAIPAUL

Childhood sometimes does pay a second visit; youth never.

MRS. JAMESON

If we could be twice young and twice old, we could correct all our mistakes.

EURIPIDES

What really shapes and conditions and makes us is somebody only a few of us ever have the courage to face: and that is the child you once were, long before formal education ever got its claws into you . . . It is those pent-up, craving children who make all the wars and all the horrors and all the art and all the beauty and discovery in life, because they are trying to achieve what lay beyond their grasp before they were five years old.

ROBERTSON DAVIES

In the midst of winter, I finally learned that there was in me an invincible summer.

ALBERT CAMUS

Fools have their second childhood, but the Great
Still keep their first, and have no second state.

WILLIAM HENRY DAVIES

we almost have forgotten that
we also are as the hands of children,
reaching through in the breath
of curiosity and being continually
borne across, the more that we are
able to give ourselves over.

WILLIAM KISTLER

It takes a long time to become young.

PABLO PICASSO

He is the happiest man who can trace an unbroken connection between the end of his life and the beginning.

JOHANN WOLFGANG VON GOETHE

Poetry begins in childhood, and the poet who can remember his or her childhood exactly has an obligation to write for children.

WILLIAM JAY SMITH

I don't know who I am or who I was. I know it less than ever. I do and I don't identify myself with myself. Everything is totally contradictory but maybe I have remained exactly as I was as a small boy of twelve.

ALBERTO GIACOMETTI

Age only matters when one is aging. Now that I have arrived at a great age, I might just as well be twenty.

PABLO PICASSO

It is better to be a young June-bug than an old bird of paradise.

MARK TWAIN

Most of what I really need to know about how to live, and what to do, and how to be, I learned in kindergarten. Wisdom was not at the top of the graduate school mountain, but there in the sandbox at nursery school. These are the things I learned: Share everything. Play fair. Don't hit people. Put things back where you found them. Clean up your own mess. Don't take things that aren't yours. Say you're sorry when you hurt somebody. Wash your hands before you eat. Flush. Warm cookies and cold milk are good for you. Live a balanced life. Learn some and think some and draw and paint and sing and dance and play and work everyday some. Take a nap every afternoon. When you go out into the world, watch for traffic, hold hands, and stick together. Be aware of wonder. Remember the little seed in the plastic cup. The roots go down and the plant goes up and nobody really knows how or why, but we are all like that. Goldfish and hamsters and white mice and even the little seed in the plastic cup—they all die. So do we. And then remember the book about Dick and Jane and the first word you learned, the biggest word of all: LOOK .

ROBERT FULGHUM

Perhaps we are our childhood still, for—as St. Augustine once said—whither should it have gone?

RAINER MARIA RILKE

Oh, grown-ups cannot understand,
  and grown-ups never will,
How short the way to fairyland
  Across the purple hill.
    ALFRED NOYES

Childhood is the small town everyone came from.
    GARRISON KEILLOR

Every baby born into the world is a finer one than the
last.
    CHARLES DICKENS

Heaven lies about us in our infancy.
    WORDSWORTH

The best smell is bread, the best savour salt, the best
love that of children.
    PROVERB

We just happen to like children.
    FRANCES BLESS (on the birth of her
    eighteenth child)

Is it possible to push a child off one's lap? Not even Goethe would be able to do so.

MILAN KUNDERA

Children are the keys of Paradise.

R. H. STODDARD

A student from the class of 1950 (Ninalee Allen Craig) recalls Joseph Campbell's respect for the creative process in the young and not so young. In Manhattan, the story goes, Mr. Campbell found himself endlessly circling the neighborhood in search of a parking space. Finally he found a spot and as he backed into it, he saw a child, body rigid, standing on the curb. The child said, 'You can't park here.'

'Why not?' said Mr. Campbell, leaning out of the window.

The child was indignant, 'Can't you see, I'm a fire hydrant,'

Naturally, Mr. Campbell drove away.

SARAH LAWRENCE ALUMNAE MAGAZINE

When the child was a child, it walked with its arms swinging. It wanted the stream to be a river, the river a torrent and this puddle to be the sea. When the child was a child, it didn't know it was a child. Everything was full of life and all life was one. When the child was a child, it had no opinions about anything. It had no habits. It sat cross-legged. It took off running, had a cowlick in its hair and didn't make a face when photographed.

From the movie *WINGS OF DESIRE*

There are only two things a child will share willingly—communicable diseases and his mother's age.

BENJAMIN SPOCK

Is nothing in life ever straight and clear, the way children see it?

ROSIE THOMAS

I think the memory of most of us can go farther back . . . than most of us suppose; just as I believe the power of observation in numbers of very young children to be quite wonderful for its closeness and accuracy.

CHARLES DICKENS

It seems to me that the presence of children is the redeeming feature in storytelling . . . Without them, it's all pleasant enough, but it's just nostalgic. And I'm not really very interested in that. For children, who have a great deal of curiosity about what happened before they came along, I'm willing to work hard.

GARRISON KEILLOR

You don't need Little League. You don't even need nine kids. Four is plenty—a pitcher, a batter, and a couple of shaggers. You can play ball all day long. My kids used to try to get me out there, but I'd just say, "Go play with your brother." If kids want to do something, they'll do it. They don't need adults to do it for them.

YOGI BERRA

My parents put a live teddy bear in my crib.

WOODY ALLEN

All our adventures were by the fireside, and all our migrations from the blue bed to the brown.

OLIVER GOLDSMITH

Alas, regardless of their doom,
The little victims play!
No sense have they of ills to come,
Nor care beyond to-day.

THOMAS GRAY

In the lives of children, God joins company with kings, superheroes, witches, monsters, friends, brothers and sisters, parents, teachers, police, fire-fighters, and on and on.

ROBERT COLES

We can keep from a child all knowledge of earlier myths, but we cannot take from him the need for mythology.

JUNG

Many children, dressed in pastels, sit around the long table. They are exhausted and overexcited from games fiercely played, some are flushed and wet, others un-naturally pale. This general agitation, and the paper party hats they wear, combine to make them appear a dinner party of debauched midgets. It is time for the cake. A huge chocolate cake in the shape of a rocket and launching pad and covered with blue and pink icing is carried in. In the hush the birthday child begins to cry. He stops crying makes a wish and blows out the candles.

PAMELA ZOLINE

Ask your child what he wants for dinner only if he is buying.

FRAN LEBOWITZ

A food is not necessarily essential just because your child hates it.

KATHERINE WHITEHOUSE

Children are all foreigners. We treat them as such.

EMERSON

Children are the great gamble. From the moment they are born, our helplessness increases. Instead of being ours to mould and shape after our best knowledge and endeavour, they are themselves. From their birth they are the centre of our lives, and the dangerous edge of existence.

JOSEPHINE HART

Tristan and Isolde were unloved only children.

W. H. AUDEN

Befiehl dem Herrn deine Wege u. hoffe auf ihn er wirds wohl machen.

Nothing is more useful than to adopt the status of a child: a child can do whatever it likes, for it is innocent and inexperienced; it need not observe the rules of social behavior, for it has not yet entered a world ruled by form; it may show its feelings, whether they are appropriate or not.

MILAN KUNDERA

When I was younger, I could remember anything, whether it had happened or not.

MARK TWAIN

Eternity is a child playing checkers.

HERACLITUS

"Did you have a happy childhood?" is a false question. As a child I did not know what happiness was, and whether I was happy or not. I was too busy being.

ALISTAIR REID

The ten-year-old gives a fair indication of the man or woman he or she is to be.

ARNOLD GESELL

Part of the reason for the ugliness of adults, in a child's eyes, is that the child is usually looking upwards, and few faces are at their best when seen from below.

GEORGE ORWELL

It is, in some ways, but a pedestrian fancy that the child exhibits. It is the grown people who make the nursery stories; all the children do is jealously to preserve the text.

ROBERT LOUIS STEVENSON

A girl of fifteen generally has a greater number of secrets than an old man.

ORTEGA Y GASSET

A trick that everyone abhors
In little girls is slamming doors.

HILAIRE BELLOC

When a healthy three-year old child says, "I love you," there is meaning in it like that between men and women who love and are in love.

D. W. WINNICOTT

A baby is an inestimable blessing and bother.
MARK TWAIN

There is no more sombre enemy of good art then the pram in the hall.
CYRIL CONNOLLY

The persons hardest to convince they're at the retirement age are children at bedtime.
SHANNON FIFE

Never have children; only grandchildren.
GORE VIDAL

Do your kids a favor—don't have any.
ROBERT ORBEN

It is dangerous to confuse your children with angels.
DAVID FYFE

Ignorance is a painless evil; so, I should think, is dirt, considering the merry faces that go along with it.
GEORGE ELIOT

Permissiveness is the principle of treating children as if they were adults; and the tactic of making sure they never reach that stage.

THOMAS SZASZ

Remember when your mother used to say, "Go to your room—"? This was a terrible penalty. Now when a mother says the same thing, a kid goes to his room. There he's got an air-conditioner, a TV set, an intercom, a shortwave radio—he's better off than he was in the first place.

SAM LEVENSON

He that spareth his rod hateth his son: but he that loveth him chasteneth him betimes.

PROVERBS 13:24

If you must hold yourself up to your children as an object lesson, hold yourself up as a warning and not as an example.

GEORGE BERNARD SHAW

Too much sugar in youth makes decayed teeth in age.

GERMAN PROVERB

The precursor of the mirror is the mother's face.

D. W. WINNICOTT

If you want to have a baby, have a new one. Don't baby the old one.

JESSAMYN WEST

Never grow a wishbone, daughter, where your backbone ought to be.

CLEMENTINE PADDLEFORD

Don't set your wit against a child.

JONATHAN SWIFT

Men are generally more careful of the breed of their horses and dogs than of their children.

WILLIAM PENN

I phoned my dad to tell him I had stopped smoking. He called me a quitter.

STEVEN PEARL

Never lend your car to anyone to whom you have given birth.

ERMA BOMBECK

Never threaten a child with a visit to the dentist.
JANE BRODY

If you strike a child, strike him only with a shoelace.
BABYLONIAN TALMUD

Any mother could perform the jobs of several air-traffic controllers with ease.
LISA ALTHER

My mother had a great deal of trouble with me but I think she enjoyed it.
MARK TWAIN

A father is a banker provided by nature.
ANONYMOUS

The affection of a father and a son are different: the father loves the person of the son, and the son loves the memory of his father.
ANONYMOUS

What was silent in the father speaks in the son; and often I found the son the unveiled secret of the father.
NIETZSCHE

In a game of chess between a father and his eight-year-old daughter, the little girl moved the pawn in the wrong direction.

"You can't do that, Sarah!" Father corrected, returning the pawn. "You have to move FORWARD."

Sarah thought for a moment, walked to the other side of the table—and moved the pawn FORWARD.

BEN ALGASE

There's a time when you have to explain to your children why they're born, and it's a marvelous thing if you know the reason by then.

HAZEL SCOT

Something you consider bad may bring out your child's talents; something you consider good may stifle them.

CHATEAUBRIAND

Before I got married I had six theories about bringing up children; now I have six children and no theories.

JOHN WILMOT, EARL OF ROCHESTER

Most of us become parents long before we have stopped being children.

MIGNON MCLAUGHLIN

Yes, the essence of every love is a child, and it makes no difference at all whether it has ever actually been conceived or born. In the algebra of love, a child is the symbol of the magical sum of two beings.

MILAN KUNDERA

Greatness of name, in the father, oftimes helps not forth, but overwhelms the son; they stand too near one another. The shadow kills the growth.

BEN JONSON

What's done to children, they will do to society.

KARL MENNINGER

How sharper than a serpent's tooth it is
To have a thankless child.

KING LEAR

It costs a great deal to be reasonable; it costs youth.

MADAME DE LA FAYETTE

The arbitrary nature of our passion for children, who reveal so little of themselves during their short stay with us, is, for many, life's great romance. But, unlike the object of our romantic love, we do not choose the child who will be our son or daughter.

JOSEPHINE HART

He followed in his father's footsteps, but his gait was somewhat erratic.

NICOLAS BENTLEY

Nothing has a stronger influence psychologically on their environment, and especially on their children than the unlived life of the parents.

JUNG

The imitativeness of our early years makes us acquire the passions of our parents, even when these passions poison our lives.

STENDHAL

Happiness is an imaginary condition formerly often attributed by the living to the dead, now usually attributed by adults to children, and by children to adults.

THOMAS SZASZ

The chief cause of human errors is to be found in prejudices picked up in childhood.

RENE DESCARTES

There are three degrees of filial piety. The highest is being a credit to our parents, the second is not disgracing them; the lowest is being able simply to support them.

CONFUCIUS

The behavior of many children suggests that their parents embarked on the sea of matrimony without a paddle.

LEONARD ROSSITER

The modern child will answer you back before you've said anything.

LAURENCE J. PETER

I stopped believing in Santa Claus when I was six. Mother took me to see him in a department store, and he asked for my autograph.

SHIRLEY TEMPLE

The first duty of young people is to become older.
    BENEDITO CROCE

All children, except one, grow up.
    PETER PAN

Let your children go if you want to keep them.
    MALCOLM FORBES

Sweet childish days, that were as long
As twenty days are now.
    WORDSWORTH

You grow up the day you have your first real laugh at
yourself.
    ETHEL BARRYMORE

You know children are growing up when they start ask-
ing questions that have answers.
    JOHN J. PLOMB

A child becomes an adult when he realizes he has a
right not only to be right but also to be wrong.
    THOMAS SZASZ

When it comes time to do your own life, you either perpetuate your childhood or you stand on it and finally kick it out from under.

ROSELLEN BROWN

All adolescents should be given a thoroughly beastly time of it, in order to leave them something to look forward to when they grow up.

RICHARD GORDON

It goes without saying that you should never have more children than you have car windows.

ERMA BOMBECK

See that he knows his childhood once again;
the wonderful, instinctive things
and the infinite circle of dark rich legend
of his ominous early years.

RILKE

What is youth except a man or woman before it is fit to be seen.

EVELYN WAUGH

Youth is a wonderful thing: what a crime to waste it on children.

GEORGE BERNARD SHAW

Remember that as a teenager you are in the last stage of your life when you will be happy to hear that the phone is for you.

FRAN LEBOWITZ

There is no landscape like the landscape of childhood, terrain at once vivid and hauntingly vague. What remains for me are dozens of images and names, faces and events, animals and objects, a light I associate with dusk, fallen leaves, the smell and feel of thick grass. My first memory is of throwing a stone at a goose floating serenely on a small pond and seeing the beautiful ripples in the water; my second is of having my hair cut.

JUDITH FREEMAN

. . .we find our childhood selves, and our present differences from those selves, in the pages of the books we long ago read as children.

WENDY LESSER

There are children playing in the street who could solve some of my top problems in physics, because they have modes of sensory perception that I lost long ago.

J. ROBERT OPPENHEIMER

As an artist grows older, he has to fight disillusionment and learn to establish the same relationship to nature as an adult as he had when he was a child.

CHARLES BIRCHFIELD

The whole of appearance is a toy.

WALLACE STEVENS

The child had every toy his father wanted.

ROBERT WHITTEN

The events of childhood do not pass, but repeat themselves like seasons of the year.

ELEANOR FARJEON

The tragedy of old age is not that we are old, but that we are young.

OSCAR WILDE

Everything else you grow out of, but you never recover from childhood.

BERYL BAINBRIDGE

A toy car is a projection of a real car, made small enough for a child's hand and imagination to grasp. A real car is a projection of a toy car, made large enough for an adult's hand and imagination to grasp.

MICHAEL FRAYN

I am married to Beatrice Salkeld, a painter. We have no children, except me.

BRENDAN BEHAN

In every real man a child is hidden that wants to play.

NIETZSCHE

Childishness follows us all the days of our life.

LA ROCHEFOUCAULD

Every adult, whether he is a follower or a leader, a member of a mass or an elite, was once a child. He was once small. A sense of smallness forms a substratum of his mind, ineradicably. His triumphs will be measured against this smallness, his defeats will substantiate it.

ERIC ERIKSON

Her words still filled his mind
As they started their journey,
Just as a mother's voice is heard
Sometimes in a man's mind
Long past childhood
Calling his name, calling him from sleep
Or from some pleasureful moment
On a foreign street
When every trace of origin seems left
And one has almost passed into a land
That promises a vision or the secret
Of one's life, when one feels almost god enough
To be free of voices, her voice
Calls out like a voice from childhood,
Reminding him he once tossed in dreams.

THE GILGAMESH

Successful careers are those that realize in man the dreams of the child.

WALLACE STEVENS

You're never too old to become younger.

MAE WEST

How old would you be if you didn't know how old you was?

SATCHEL PAIGE

I don't know what I may seem to the world, but, as to myself, I seem to have been only like a boy playing on the sea shore, and diverting myself now and then finding a smoother pebble or a prettier shell than ordinary, whilst the great ocean of truth lay all undiscovered before me.

SIR ISAAC NEWTON

It may be that we have to lose that knowledge and understanding which children have and then perhaps it comes back to us through living experience and wisdom.

LOUIS BROMFIELD

It was only in my forties that I started feeling young.

HENRY MILLER

You can't help getting older, but you don't have to get old.

GEORGE BURNS

I'll tell ya how to stay young: Hang around with older people.

BOB HOPE

The secret of staying young is to live honestly, eat slowly and lie about your age.

LUCILLE BALL

The trick is growing up without growing old.

CASEY STENGEL

CHILD
was designed by Hudson Studio
Ossining, New York